NATURAL SCIENCE

POEMS BY

JOYCE SCHMID

GLASS LYRE PRESS

Design & Layout: Steven Asmussen
Cover Art: From Yashina S, Gubin S, Maksimovich S, Yashina A, Gakhova E,
Gilichinsky D. Regeneration of whole fertile plants from 30,000-y-old fruit tissue
buried in Siberian permafrost. Proc Natl Acad Sci U S A. 2012 Mar 6;109(10):4008-
13. doi: 10.1073/pnas.1118386109. Epub 2012 Feb 21. PMID: 22355102; PMCID:
PMC3309767. Figure 3, Photograph C. Used with the gracious permission of *The Pro-
ceedings of the National Academy of Sciences* (PNAS) , journal of the National Academy
of Sciences.

Author Photograph: Audra Miller, Miller Studios.

Glass Lyre Press, LLC
P.O. Box 2693
Glenview, IL 60025
www.GlassLyrePress.com

Natural Science

CONTENTS

LIFE SCIENCE

PHYSICAL SCIENCE

LIFE SCIENCE

Hyalinobatrachium yaku

Glass Frog

My home is in cloud forests,
where you'll never find me—

tiny, green to the bone—
translucent skin.

If you discover me, beware:
I wear a dagger.

I will never let you see
the writhing of my naked heart.

DICTYOSTELIUM DISCOIDEUM

When food is scarce
or when the temperature is wrong,
slime mold amoebas band in groups

to form a single slug-like thing.
Without a brain,
this slug thing creeps toward light

until it finds a promised land,
and stops.
Then each amoeba

marches out of slug formation,
and rejoins its neighbors
to make fruiting bodies,

graceful as budding tulips.
Some amoebas choose
to be the roots

and stalks that die,
while others clamber up
to be the fruit.

TRILOBITES

"Some 365 million years ago, eyeless trilobites marched across the seafloor in single file."

—*Nicholas St. Fleur, NY Times*

I can't see anything,
but I can sense you there
in front of me

and I am drawn to follow you
wherever you may go,
with you in front of me

and someone else behind me,
trekking somewhere,
though I don't know where.

All I know
is that you're there
and I am following,

a darkness holding us,
and somewhere—
high above us

in another kind of world—
an unimaginable
light.

WING SONG

African Broadbill

Be song,
don't sing song.
Let the motion
of your being sing.
Fly,

and in the act of flying,
be.
And I will know you
by the music of your wings
and find you

flying green ellipses
branch
      to
           branch
among the leaves.

ESCHRICHTIUS ROBUSTUS

Gray Whale

The sea is giving up its whales,
thirteen of them this year near San Francisco,
and it's only May.
People crawl all over them
and try to understand:
they died of hunger,
or they died of being hit by ships,
or maybe of an overdose of trash.

The why is less important, only that they're dead.
The earth cannot support its giants any more.
Dear children, say goodbye.
You missed the dinosaurs.
They may have looked like birds
and danced like birds
and given rise to birds.
But could they sing?

Some whales can sing,
the sound more cow than bird,
more like a slide trombone.

I've never seen a whale or heard one,
but I've seen a flock of birds that swirled
above a whale, and recognized the subtle spray
as evidence a whale was there.
There's nothing subtle here,
a carcass on a beach
enclosing secrets, like an egg,
its thin shell filled
with emptiness.

Eastern Emerald Elysia

These little sea slugs
start their lives red-brown,
in shells, exposed
to predators against
the green of sea.

They suckle algae
and they change:
the green they swallow
dyes their bodies green.
Their shells dissolve,

their bodies morph—
and they are ambulating leaves.
They feed on light,
their dim capacity for green
fulfilled. Both animal

and plant but only animal
at birth, they blur
the boundaries
that can't quite separate
the kingdoms of the earth.

Silene stenophylla

Regrown from the Pleistocene

The petals are much narrower,
more splayed, and yet they look
as fresh as modern campion,
as clean. The thirty-two millennia
that lie between the generation
and the germination of its seed
have seen the glaciers melt,
the wooly mammoths die.

Is the little plant dismayed
to wake uprooted from prehistory,
surrounded by machines?
Or does it celebrate its resurrection
with a shiver
of its leaves, a glowing
of its flower, a stirring
in its fruit?

PSITTACUS ERITHACUS

Petra, Congo parrot, said:
Alexa, all the lights on.
And Alexa said OK—

and there was light.

Standing on her perch,
a cross made out of reddish logs,
the parrot saw that it was good.

And then the she said:
Alexa, all the lights off,

and darkness covered
all the surface of the deep.

The parrot, filled with joy
at separating darkness
from the light,

called her faithful servant
once again and told her
in a low, un-birdlike voice:

I love you.

Note: Story found in DailyMail.com Reporter

Firehawks

Imagine Noah's dove,
the olive leaf on fire.
Now think of whistling kites
and brown Australian falcons,
branches burning in their beaks.

Some say the aborigines who claim
they've seen the firehawks
are spreading myth,

but you and I know otherwise—
we've seen them fly,
we've seen the flicker in their eyes,
these birds who set the ground ablaze—
we've seen the flames—
we've seen the spreading of the fire.

THE IDLE ANTS

Not the ones who clean the colony,
not the ones who go outside
to fight or hunt for food,

and not the queen, who labors
in her chamber,
too exhausted to remember

flying in the sun.
I mean the other ants,
the ones who stand and sense

the universe,
who broadcast beauty
all throughout the nest

to shield their sisters
from the black of space,
the raw, incinerating stars.

PHYSICAL SCIENCE

CHAOS THEORY I: FRACTALS

Clouds and coastlines are,
like trees
and other branching things,
self-similar—
their shapes repeat,
and are the same
reduced or magnified.
Which natural shapes
repeating to infinity
reveal the shape of God?

CHAOS THEORY II: STRANGE ATTRACTOR

"...oft did we grow
To be two chaoses...."
—*John Donne*

Love is a basin of attraction.
Its every contour leads to you,
each time differently,
and each time ending
in a different place,
the place you are.
My pathways form a never-ending pattern,
a spiral of spirals of spirals,
like hurricanes and human hearts,
unpredictable by human brains,
known only by the force
that set it all in motion,
drawing me
to you.

CHAOS THEORY III: THE SUM OF MANY TINY PULSES

The fractal of our lives
is written on my face,
but you are kind
and say that you don't see it.
How did you,
a continent away,
find me?
Was it the lavender in bloom,
in perfect blue perfume
to draw the butterfly
that stoked a hurricane
and whirled it
out among the stars?

The Carbon Atom

Carbon has a choice.

Alone, it can be coal
releasing fire
as it disappears

or diamond
flashing
hard, unliving light.

Or it can stretch its arms
to oxygen and hydrogen
and come alive.

MOON ROCKS

Houston Space Center

I've seen many things in glass cases
but never before
the moon.

Men survived the push of fire,
claustrophobic space,
to plant a flag
and leftover machinery
on the virgin moon.
Now they are heroes.

And the moon?

Chunks and pieces,
grey and brown rocks,
gravel and sand,
spread for all to see
in cases made of glass.

SPACE

stars gravitate   apart   whole continents

are drifting   ice-shelves shatter into shards

where is   the universe i knew   the one

that stayed the same   i am too small

to feel it change *and yet it moves*   its passion

growing   as it dies   you smile

i reach for you   why   should i be

surprised to find   that you are floating

farther   from me too

Note: "And yet it moves" is a phrase attributed to Galileo Galilei.

IMAGINARY MASS

Will the empty space that once was me
be teeming with exotic matter
leading to another time and place?

Will you, searching everywhere for me,
feel a perturbation in the air
and be attracted there, not knowing why?

Will you leap into the wormhole
and go after me, and find me
as you've always found me-- lost,

but knowing you will come for me?

Quantum Entanglement

We've been flying in a ray of light,
moving at the highest limit of velocity.

Now our beam of light is squeezed,
compressed inside a crystal of pure time.

When at last we splat in the detector
made to chart our quantum links,

the Scientist will find us tangled up together,
you and me so closely bound

that He will need to measure only one of us
to know the other's properties.

Rainbow

Why must I be broken,
spread across the sky
from earth to earth,

an unprotected show of color,
visible from everywhere,
I who was invisible as air?

My bright anatomy is my affair.
Just close your eyes a moment
while I dress, it won't take long.

The clouds will cover me,
the rain will dry.
I'll change

and reappear
as ordinary light.

Low Ionization Emission-Line Region

Even galaxies have life spans.
Over time,
the swirling firebirds
stop laying stars
and die,
to whirl about the universe forever,
red and dead.

But if two red, dead galaxies collide,
a miracle occurs:
both come alive.
They open out their fiery tails again
and spin in blinding astral passion,
breeding gaggles
of enormous stars.

Acknowledgments

Deepest thanks to the editors of the journals where the following poems first appeared:

Chautauqua—Dictyostelium discoideum (As "Swarm Intelligence")
Comstock Review—Wing Song, Eschrichtius robustus
Critica—Firehawks; Hyalinobatrachium yaku (As "Glass Frog")
Duck Lake Journal—Trilobites (As "Under a Vanished Ocean")
Full-color Catalog of The Microbiomes, Corvalis Arts Center, 2017— Eastern Emerald Elysia
La Piccioletta Barca—Silene stenophylla (As "Grown From the Pleistocene")
Fourth River—Psyttacus Erithacus (As "Bird and Machine")
Missouri Review—The Idle Ants
Salt Poetry Journal—Imaginary Mass; Low Ionization Emission-Line Region

About the Author

Joyce Schmid is a grandmother and psychotherapist living in Palo Alto, California, with her husband of over half a century. After graduation from Harvard College in History and Literature, she studied Russian Literature at Columbia Graduate School of Arts and Sciences, where she was twice awarded their Pushkin Prize for poetry translation. Her work has most recently appeared in *Salt, Passager, New Ohio Review, Bridport Prize Anthology 2023, The Husdon Review*, and other journals and anthologies.

Glass Lyre Press

exceptional works to replenish the spirit

Glass Lyre Press is an independent literary publisher interested in technically accomplished, stylistically distinct, and original work. Glass Lyre seeks diverse writers that possess a dynamic aesthetic and an ability to emotionally and intellectually engage a wide audience of readers.

Glass Lyre's vision is to connect the world through language and art. We hope to expand the scope of poetry and short fiction for the general reader through exceptionally well-written books, which evoke emotion, provide insight, and resonate with the human spirit.

Poetry Collections
Poetry Chapbooks
Select Short & Flash Fiction
Anthologies

www.GlassLyrePress.com

Made in the USA
Monee, IL
17 April 2025

15654466R00023